The Writing Lesson
Stories and Poems

Ann Rousseau

ISBN-13: 9780692125243 (Custom Universal)
ISBN-10: 0692125248

Edited by Daryl Miller Salomons
Cover Art by Jeanne Eleck

Knowing
Things change,
I remain fixed
On this unsteady rock,
This abundance
Undeserved.

Ann Rousseau

Contents

Beginning

Later

And Then...

Foreword

This is not a memoir. While much of the content of these poems and stories is based on personal experience, I changed some details and the sequence of events. In some places, I created particular moments to serve the story. For instance, in "The Journey," my mother – not my grandmother – lived in New York City. While I had taken that train ride now and then, much of the emotional content of the story related to bus rides I took from Fairfield to Stratford, Connecticut, in order to attend ballet classes. I had to transfer buses at the central bus depot in Bridgeport, and on the return trip, in downtown Bridgeport – often when it was getting dark. I also drew upon an experience of being followed when visiting my mother in the city.

Perception plays a part in writing. Relationships, similarly, are complex and subject to interpretation. The stories and poems included here represent "traces of recollection, splinters of experience, fragments of feeling."

I wish to thank Jeanne Eleck for her wonderful cover art. I am also appreciative of those who have offered kind words, especially Daryl and Jeff for their continued encouragement and support.

Ann Rousseau

Beginning

"A fatherless girl grows up thinking that everything is possible and nothing is safe."
                    Mary Gordon

Gray Gull

Switching weight to the other foot,
A gray gull ruffles his feathers and
Casts a shiny glass eye toward
Main Street waking below

Where shopkeepers with rings of jangling keys
And shoppers with darting eyes
Rush to market,
Breathing quickly.

The lone gull
Presses closer to the weathered eve,
Beholding the colors of daily noise;
Then blinking as though to clear his eye,
Looks away
In search of real treasure.

The Writing Lesson

Standing on tiptoes, she carefully unfolded her fingers and pushed the coins across the glass counter. The clerk didn't return her smile but impatiently stood by while she touched, turned, and examined each plastic pencil. The red one was too dark. The green one was possible. She held the blue apart; its crystalline brilliance shone jewel-like. It was right. She would purchase beauty for her father on the occasion of his birthday. He would never see it. He was blind.

A year before, the little girl in blue overalls had made dusty "stepfoots" in the sandy gravel as she walked hand in hand with the man in dark glasses who saw only shadows. The early September air was rich; the first lines of red and amber laced green leaves in the yellow light of late afternoon.

"Tell me what you see, Dolly. You will have to be my eyes now." Her first writing lesson.

She didn't know what to say. She saw trees. She saw some red leaves, some green leaves. Even then, she felt the inadequacy of her words. She would have to do better.

As she grew, she struggled. She looked more carefully at things around her. She collected words, phrases, and images and kept them in a box under her desk. She read more. She wrote more. Occasionally, a phrase came together but it was never good enough. No matter how detailed, the writing seemed flat. She seemed to be describing the outsides of things. Something was missing.

She could embellish the writing by drawing from a common well of words and experiences. The reader would

3

understand the difference between the delicate blue of bird's egg and the radiant blue of a cornflower because he had experienced "delicate." He had experienced "radiant." The writing still seemed incomplete.

One day, sitting at her desk in the afternoon quiet, the woman drew forth another sheet of paper. The window was open and the sun warmed her face as she replaced the cartridge in her pen and held the point tentatively to the empty page. The words that fell summoned only traces of a recollection, splinters of an experience, fragments of a feeling; yet, the shadow of beauty pleased her. The curtains hovered like snow, and the page ruffled as if to escape her grasp. She snatched it back to add one last line: "For my father."

To Begin

The sock drawer organized,
I have no excuse not
To begin.
It is indeed joyous
To begin,
To follow my heart finally
To begin.

The notebook calls;
The laundry beckons.

Learn How to Fly

Buy a ticket on Delta;
Jump off a roof;
Strap yourself to an eagle.

If one isn't around,
Take feathers from an old pillow,
Paste them on to your arms
In nine careful rows.
Use beeswax as Daedalus did.

Wait for a big wind,
Perhaps an address from
A presidential candidate.

If you do get aloft,
Remember not to fly too high.
Poets as well as manbirds
Burn out.

Be Careful

Do not speak quickly.
There is risk in being wrong.
Unlike writing, which can be revised,
Spoken words cannot be called back.
More permanent than
The written page,
Words fly out
Fly away
Fly far from our control.

Making Meaning

Interesting we arrive
at places not so distant worlds
beyond where we thought we'd be
but what did we really know
and how could we really when
all we were
we were then so who

are we now
carried gently softly
a wave's passenger taking
time to raise our heads
occasionally to notice
where we are to consider
uncharted islands we may visit
tomorrow

who would have thought but why not
and if vessels of the hour
why then anguish
let it go give it up let it happen
see
what is to discover.

Crisp Morning

On this clear morning,
Stems bend,
Blossom heads heavy with dew.
Fields of thick green
Carpet roadsides.

I float along familiar paths.
Mists of memory cloud my lens.
Bones of the past rattle underfoot.

Long ago
I knew this place.

Big Yellow Bus

From the edge of the world
We would shiver to Katonah,
The big black wheels
Crunching to a stop
As Nancy Marks,
Toast in hand,
Jacket flapping,
Flew down her long, icy driveway.

Lurching forward, wide-eyed,
We bumped along country roads as
Cheryl told of Charlie Chipmunk's adventures.
Susie giggled at her plan to play "married" at recess.
Billy, unaware, gazed out through dusty windows
While his one true love stole secret glances.

Lumbering onto
Pressed snow fields,
The big yellow bus stopped
To deposit its noisy cargo.

Bumping and jostling,
The throngs pressed forward,
Spilling eagerly onto a slippery playground.
The journey over –
Not soon enough for all
But one.

Walk at River's Edge

We followed the stones,
Jagged outcroppings of rock
Along the river bank.

We jumped from step to step
As children jump.
There were missteps,
Reckless leaps,
Graceless landings.

Granite sparkled
Solid beneath our feet.
Shards of light pierced
Murky waters below.

We shared the journey.
The joy of the moment was
All.

The Journey

This gray morning, she waited on the Greenwich train platform as snow fell around her. She was ten years old – a big girl. She would be able to travel to her grandma's apartment in New York City by herself. There was no reason to be afraid. Thousands of people rode trains every day; for some, boarding the train was as much a part of a morning routine as brushing teeth.

The little girl would often accompany her mother from where they lived in Connecticut to the apartment in New York City. Much of what she knew of the world lay in those two places that were joined by the twenty-four mile stretch of track.

On bone-chilling winter mornings, wind cut through her coat and no amount of stamping would keep her feet warm. She would follow her mother to the train station, placing her boots carefully atop the wet, slushy barricades created by heavy-breathing plows, taking measured steps up icy stairs to the platform. It was better on warm spring mornings. She loved how the sunlight would filter through the fresh green leaves to make shadows that danced at her feet. On those days, time seemed to pass quickly as she paced, passing the colorful theater posters that lined the station.

On this morning, clouds of snow swirled and fell in a cold mist to her face. Soon she heard the signal in the station announcing the approaching train. As her mom had always warned her, she stepped back behind the yellow line on the pavement. The first cars of the train barreled by, ruffling her scarf. She tightened her hold on her backpack as the train slowed to a stop.

Doors slid open and those around her rushed to enter. She waited and at the last moment, stepped aboard. Once in the car, she turned sideways to pass beyond the giants who crowded the entry way and made her way down the aisle, keeping her eyes to the floor as she moved. There were two empty seats near the center of the car. She fell onto the window seat as the train lurched forward. She placed her backpack on the seat beside her.

Trains were friendlier than buses that would jar you, make you carsick if you tried to read. Unlike trains, they lacked the familiar dust and soot that refused to be swept away, that hid in the corners of window panes and beneath seats of old leather, traces of former passengers and years of transit. They lacked the comfort of history, of connection. Turning to the window, she noticed that the snow was falling harder. Cars and buses might face delays, but the train would continue.

With each stop, more commuters whooshed aboard, bringing in the stress and cold of the morning. Each juggled newspapers, cases, and paper cups brimming with steaming coffee. The car was crowded. A few stood in the aisle. No one disturbed the backpack on the nearby seat.

On morning trains, there was always the comfort of familiar rituals: the greetings exchanged, the cups held firmly over rough stretches of track – lifted two minutes beyond the Port Chester station, five seconds before the curve in the track near New Rochelle – the shared moments of community.

She closed her eyes and was comforted by the rocking. The occasional slows and the slapping noise as other trains sped by made a strange yet predictable music. A conductor strolled though the cars, rebounding from the shoulders of seats, struggling to keep balance, the clicking of tickets adding to the music of the morning – some phrases of melody interrupted by the brakes shrieking against cold track.

When she opened her eyes, he was there. Her backpack was on the floor. His black hoodie was drawn close around his face. She noticed a tattoo along the edge of his wrist, most of it covered by the cuff of his jacket. He didn't speak. Much of his face was hidden but what was revealed seemed stone-like, gray and frozen. He seemed to radiate cold. She lifted her backpack to her lap and clutched it to herself.

Perhaps he was a student at a city school. Perhaps he was visiting someone. She had no reason to be afraid. She pushed back her sleeve and looked at her watch. Soon the train ride would be over. She looked to the window; the snow was heavier yet, a thick covering on the roofs and roads.

Suddenly, the train pulled into darkness. When she turned toward the window, she saw only her own face. The metal screamed as it held fast to the curved track. She was jarred from side to side. Finally, the train crisscrossed the maze of tracks and groaned to a halt at its final stop.

As though by silent signal, papers and cases were gathered, clothes straightened. She stood, adjusted her backpack, and waited for an opportunity to step into the aisle.

Once on the platform, she was carried forward by the wave of rushing commuters. She struggled to keep up. At the end of the stone corridor, they emerged into the great domed arena with its arching starry sky, the center of the universe, and were met by another symphony of sounds – footsteps, announcements.

13

Later in the day, it would be different. Crowds would thin and the pace would slow. Tourists would take time to circle the great center of marble and brass that caged the information-givers. They would browse the newspaper stands and discount gift shops. They might seat themselves on the raised thrones and put their leather shoes on brass soles to be spit-shined. Now the throngs made their deliberate and fast departure, some descending into subway tubes through shiny windmills while others pressed on through gates with metal fingers meshed to allow exit only.

She knew her route. She would climb the great winding staircase that opened onto a platform of waiting yellow checkered cabs and then turn right to follow several blocks to Fifth. There she would walk briskly the many blocks until she came to 72nd Street where she would turn the corner, enter the lobby, and buzz number 2B.

She braced herself as she went through the doors. Snow was still falling heavily, making it hard to see. The noises of the city were not muffled by the soft white. She struggled to balance her backpack, readjusted her scarf, and started on her way.

It wasn't until she had walked about a block and a half that she had a sense she was being watched. People hurried past her, each person focused on his own activity, his own destination. She turned and looked back. The wind whipped her hair into her eyes; she squinted to see more clearly. She wasn't sure. She thought she saw a hunched figure with a black hood moving along behind her.

Was it possible? She felt her heartbeat quicken beneath her heavy coat. Her thoughts were racing. Perhaps it wasn't the person from the train. It could have been just a coincidence that he was walking in the same direction. She stumbled, her footing lost against the curb. When she regained her balance, her hands suddenly felt colder. She walked faster.

She decided to cross the street, hoping that he would continue on. She knew she was supposed to cross at the corner, but this was an emergency. A taxi cab blared an objection as she darted across.

Safely to the other side, she glanced back. He had crossed behind her. The figure shrouded in snow seemed to be gaining on her. As his pace increased, so did her sense of panic. What if she stopped and confronted him? What if she asked him what he wanted? She was breathing heavily. She had no numbers to call, no plan.

She hurried but kept her eyes to the pavement, not wanting another misstep. She looked up suddenly, avoiding a near collision with a large woman in a green coat. She glanced back. The figure was still following, but seemed at a greater distance. She was momentarily reassured but walked more quickly. It was a distance to her destination and she was already winded.

At last, she turned the corner and was within reach of her grandmother's apartment building. There was no time to look back. She pulled at the heavy door and rushed to the wall of apartment doorbells. Her trembling hands pushed the button next to Apartment 2B. "Grandma, I'm here. Please let me in. Hurry!"

Almost immediately, the buzzer rang and the door to the inner lobby clicked open. She didn't wait for an elevator; she ran up the stairs, taking two in each stride. Her grandmother was waiting with the door open. "What's the matter?"

Once inside, still panting, she unzipped and threw off her snow-covered jacket. Brushing the snow from her hair, the story of her trip on the train and the mysterious man in the hoodie gushed from her as one explosive sentence. Her grandmother took her jacket. "There, there! It's all right now!" She was safe.

Later while they were having tea, her grandmother reminded her of her very active imagination and they laughed that she had been so frightened, that she had created a drama for what should have been a routine trip.

Her grandmother rose slowly and brought the teacups to the kitchen. The girl looked out the window and down onto the street. People continued to hurry by. How silly she had been. Snow was falling more heavily now. The city was so beautiful when it was covered with snow.

Just beyond her line of sight, someone waited, glancing up occasionally, shifting foot to foot to keep warm.

Things My Mother Taught Me:
 Messages from Unwritten Stories

Always try to wear my hair in a style that shows off my small ears.

The ultimate compliment is when someone says that something makes me look taller.

Being neat, clean, and organized is more important than almost anything.

It's better when you wait.

It is acceptable to say something nasty to someone as long as you say it in a nice way.

It is important to always do my best, work hard, and be thought of as a "lovely person."

Richard Nixon was a wonderful person with a lovely wife. The press and the "damned Democrats" said mean things and ruined his life.

If fruits or vegetables make you sick, they probably came from another country.

Stay away from the entire West Side of New York because it's dangerous.

My mother loves me more than anyone and has always been and will always be proud of me.

Clown

Who has ever loved a clown?
Yet he prepares,
Paints on a smile,
Stumbles in big shoes.
Often a sad face hides beneath
Greasepaint.

Who has ever loved a clown?
Yet he needs,
He hopes,
He proclaims to all that life
Can be light
Can be simple
Can be sweet.

Later

"The wound is the place
where the Light enters you."

Rumi

Two Days

One sunny day,
Toddlers and puppies romp in high grass.
Friends labor heavy boxes up creaking stairs.
Shutters will remain unpainted.
Birds will flutter undisturbed.

Another day,
She scrambles among webs and spiders,
A last check of the attic before leaving,
Not enough time to find the wedding dress.
Things of value are left behind.

Hurt

I have been here before
Where the ruffian's cuff cuts
And I flow crimson to the touch.
His words dance and weave among
The shattered pieces that were once me.
It still hurts.

Loss

It's too soon for eulogy.
My arms are still warm.

To have touched if for a moment only,
To have heard your song and sung it,
To have found a home and lost it,
Shatter and spinter what remains.

Part of me will certainly be
Buried with the loss.

Familiar Story

I have turned the stone in my palm often enough
And not claimed to know it.

I knew of the wife who left,
The home disrupted,
The child torn away.

I knew the story
But not the man.

The Stranger

A space between lip and beard,
The shape of a finger,
The length of a thigh,
Contours once more familiar
Than my own.
I wait without stirring
For some familiar gesture
From the stranger.

It wasn't you.
You never would have worn
A leather watchband.

Shannon

Every child is an only child,
Nurtured among others,
Fed by a common stream,
Her universe unique.

Cherished as a holy gift,
Her father's joy and light,
She receives his best, his worst,
This parent's love complete.

Every child is an only child, who
Following her separate star,
Takes his whole heart with her
When she leaves,
His whole heart with her
When she leaves.

In memory of Bill Lowney

Rehearsal

This is another rehearsal,
another chance to witness
last days.

We surround the bed.

Her hands,
blue with insult,
tremble.
Her eyes,
clouded with despair,
look back to happier days.

All speak of
tomorrows
and hopes
and plans.

All wonder
how much time remains:
how many days,
how many hours –
for her
for us.

The Teacher

She stands erect,
A manual of correct answers
Pressed securely against
Her freshly ironed shirt –
A wall of crisp paper and cotton.

Revision

The same page,
Loved one day,
Loathed the next.

The eyes have changed,
Glazed before,
Aware today.

If it were good,
What would it be?

Try this.
Play with that.

The page remains –
Anemic.

What more can be done?
The teacher within
Has left the building.

Discretion

While sipping wine
Discreetly,
She listens to someone,
Well-intentioned and of gentle spirit,
Offer up,
Just for the sake of discussion,
A memory –
A damaging classroom incident,
An insensitive teacher,
A program found wanting.

Smiling
Discreetly,
She listens with reasonable grace.
She sympathizes,
Breathing quietly but deeply.

His venting over,
The flames unfanned,
The speaker moves on
To another subject.

She will not defend
All teachers,
All (political group),
All (ethnic group),
All (religious group),
All (national group.)

Why then
When one is cut,
Does she bleed?

On Notice

"This is the way a cancer behaves, Mrs. Rousseau. It creates its own food source." The doctor said something about more blood vessels, something about early detection and the glories of modern medicine. I didn't hear much. My grandmother's cancers had begun with breast cancer. Someone had said, "She's riddled with it." "Riddled"... an interesting word.

The doctor was still speaking. "After the surgery, depending on the kind of cancer, we can discuss follow-up treatments. We could recommend chemotherapy, radiation, or both." He was speaking clinically; I sensed that he expected me to appreciate his candor, his professionalism. My cystic, "lumpy," dense breasts made detection of any cancers difficult. The doctor continued, "Right now, let's not get ahead of ourselves. It could be nothing. There could be other reasons for these abnormalities. I see this every day. I recommend that you go ahead with your trip to Mexico. When you return, we will schedule a needle biopsy and take it from there."

I didn't see much of Mexico, other than the cracked windshields of taxis. Every taxi we took seemed to have a cracked windshield. I noticed how the tablecloth accidentally caught fire when they brought the propane tank to the table to present the specialty dessert. On a "booze cruise," after I had drunk a significant amount of tequila, I remember looking around and wondering if I could find a doctor on board who would perform the surgery right then and there so I wouldn't have to think about it anymore.

We arrived home to bitter weather. The needle biopsy came back inconclusive. Surgery was scheduled within the month.

I told myself that I would "take care of business," do whatever was necessary. I had never really liked my hair anyway. I went back to teaching. I did the outsides of things. I was there, but I really wasn't there. It seemed that even breathing took effort. I couldn't eat. My stomach was always upset. I couldn't sleep. *This is the way a cancer behaves, Mrs. Rousseau.*

I told the doctor that I was having trouble getting through the days. The doctor put his hand on my arm. "I'm sorry. It's not always fair."

I decided to write about it. I picked up the pencil.

"There is a time, most people say, when a person will try to bargain with God."

"Once I thought I knew death; I just knew about death. I carry it now as a presence within me, an unwanted and unloved child."

Really! What melodrama!

What would it matter if I wrote about this or not? What did it matter that I had worked so hard on the garden? I had worried about choosing just the right colors, the right furniture, the right accessories. I had spent hours lost in books. What did it matter if I understood that last essay, that last poem?

I dropped the pencil.

Since Danbury Hospital didn't have the kind of MRI equipment needed, I was to report to a facility a few miles away, across the state line in New York. There, technicians, using an open MRI machine, would insert wires into the problem area to pinpoint the exact location. I pictured myself impaled, with lances protruding from my breast. I would then be transported to the hospital for surgery. After this, doctors would determine if additional surgeries would be needed.

It was cold that day; the parking lot was slippery. My husband put his arm around me. "You know I would change places with you if I could."

Once inside, I was still chilled. I couldn't stop trembling. They brought me a cup containing a small pill ... Valium, I supposed. Tequila would have been better.

They completed the procedure and moved me to the vehicle that would transport me to the hospital. I discovered that the driver and the attendant were new to the job and didn't know the location of Danbury Hospital. By that time, the pill had kicked in; I didn't mind taking the scenic route. I did mind, however, that the delay meant I missed my appointed time for the operating room. I had to wait on a stretcher in the hall for almost two more hours...more time to think. A kind and well-meaning nurse told me about her own breast surgery. She didn't offer false hope. She held my hand.

I awoke to calypso music. The doctor stood at the foot of the bed. "Good news, Mrs. Rousseau. We didn't find any cancer. The increase in blood vessels was probably due to additional cystic activity. Get some rest now." I did.

On the ride home, I noticed how the snow sparkled. I didn't care if that student had finally done his homework. I didn't care if the dog had chewed a hole in the couch cushion.

When my husband – who once made me promise not to tell anyone if he ever developed hemorrhoids because George Brett had gone public and was forever known for his condition and not his stellar baseball career – toasted to my health with his buddies by telling them, "My wife has lumpy breasts. She thought she was dying, but she's going to be all right," I didn't care. And if one of them ever wondered what "lumpy breasts" looked like or even sneaked a furtive glance on the next occasion just to see which boob was larger, I could say, without a doubt, that I just didn't care.

Losing Myself

I am losing myself
Piece by piece –
Slice from breast,
Nerve from foot,
Chunk from nose –
Small subtractions
From the ample supply.

I touch the places and
Feel what used to be –
Flesh without feeling,
Substance without spirit.

I celebrate what remains
And await the next cut.

Seedlings

Our battered selves occasionally
Forget our dying
Long enough to deal in life-making.

Seedlings spring up
At the foot of
Straw-brittle reeds.

Furry Children

Whenever I think back to the dogs we have had in the past, it is always of the good times – the walks in Vermont, the evenings by the fire, the family holidays. It was just by chance I recently happened upon some older journal entries that brought back other, more trying times with some of these furry family members.

Whenever the noise of fireworks began, our Labrador retriever Barlow became desperate to be somewhere else. He was a resourceful dog, especially smart. It was unfortunate that he suffered so when there were loud noises. When a hot air balloon passed over our house one morning, Barlow insisted on getting into the shower with me!

The Fourth of July was particularly stressful for him. One year, we were going to a picnic. Following the vet's advice, we decided to tranquilize Barlow and confine him to an area of the house where he could do the least damage.

When we arrived home, he ran toward us, wagging his tail in greeting. It was more a knowing wag than a tranquil one. We had been foiled once again: Barlow had managed to move a small chest of drawers to escape, leaving a path of damage in his wake. Had he swallowed the cookie dough but concealed the little yellow pill in his cheek, only to spit it out later? He was a clever dog. It could be that no tranquilizer would have prevented his panic. We were thankful that his particular behavior was limited to loud noises and this one particular holiday.

If we had problems trying to calm and outwit Barlow, things could have been worse if our other dog Beau had suffered this anxiety. An eighty-pound mass of muscle, he could hardly be contained under normal circumstances. Beau would bound headlong into the bushes during a simple game of catch. He was like a middle school student whose body outweighed his brain. Lacking Barlow's guile, Beau would exhibit determination in less destructive ways. We never did figure out how he climbed over the upright piano we used as a barricade to confine him to the kitchen.

Like furry children, the dogs had become permanent family members. We would continue to live around them. They constantly provided valuable lessons: one should never get too attached to material possessions; properties with ponds and babbling brooks are not necessarily desirable; a white kitchen floor is not always the best choice. My husband learned that life could be less stressful if he were flexible enough to accommodate spontaneous repair jobs, and our teenaged daughter found out that there were boys in the world who had dogs that smelled worse than ours – and that such boys could feel comfortable in our home.

The Basic Yellow Dog

My terrycloth robe seemed especially thin that morning as I padded across the chilled tile to the back sliders that led to the deck. Three hungry cats huddled near the door. The sky was turning light. In a few short weeks, it would be dark at this hour, and the three would leave powdery tracks when they burst in upon my morning and scampered to their bowls.

He was not at my side, his big yellow body pressing against my robe. I smiled, recalling his patience with the cats, this good old dog, "your basic yellow dog" as I had once described him to a friend. He would yawn and stretch, his wagging end raised in play as the cats scrambled in; then he would meander out to the edge of the woods. He was as much a part of my routine as the sound of the shower in another part of the house.

On this day, I was aware of the space by my side. It often seemed that I carried the spaces in my life around with me, as though these losses were real things that would cling to the side of my robe or rise unexpectedly in the midst of some happy moment.

I would turn from weeding to a rustle among the leaves and think that perhaps it was Barlow running through the woods, returning from one of his thieving missions. He would be happy; his head would drop and eyes peer to the side mischievously as he placed the child's coat or the baseball bat or a small boot at my feet. With apologies, I would face the blonde-headed toddler and her older brother when they appeared at the front door to inquire if, by chance, I had found a missing sneaker or baseball glove in my yard.

When the neighborhood mobilized for Halloween, my memory would once again open the door to squeals of delight as goblins and princesses laughed to see their four-footed friend dressed up as Bucky Dent, the Yankees' star shortstop. Despite the elastic that held it, the baseball cap would slip down over his eyes as he pranced among his fans in the hopes of some candy.

He was the only dog in the neighborhood who was universally allowed in houses. He could even let himself into one family's home; the teenage son awoke one morning to find that he shared his bed with a big, snoring dog. One couple without a pet of their own stocked their kitchen with dog biscuits. When out walking, people who seldom spoke to us would shout, "Hello, Barlow."

Lifting my coffee mug, I looked out the window at the yellow and red leaves stirring in the backyard. Some trees had lost all but a few. Throughout the winter, I would carry the image of this brisk autumn morning, and with it, the warm and loving memory of "the basic yellow dog" that had so enriched the lives of many.

Ballgame

What is it about a ball
Soaring onto green or
Out of the park that
So enchants,
Feeds our dreams, and
Rouses our spirits
More than
Loftier achievements of
Mind and soul?

Benched

The bench is cold.
He looks to others
Lost in the game,
Then to the ground where
He drags a twig along the dirt,
Spelling out a word
Known only to him.

Pride

He carries pride like inherited currency,
Claiming the accomplishments of his ancestors.
He swells,
Puffs up,
Defines himself by those who
Came before,
Celebrating what he chooses to see.

His flag soars.
He polishes the medals of historic victory.
He sifts,
Selects,
Savors,
Careful to disregard
The darker moments.

He sees the details of history
Without understanding the lessons.

Considering Prison

"If you want to see your husband alive again, don't hang up!"
We were separated. I hung up.

It wasn't that I wanted to see harm come to my ex; I was just
suspicious of anyone who began a call with a threat. For all I
knew, the call may have come from an inept telemarketer
who would follow that question with, "Of course, you want to
see him alive! And he would be *really* alive on a wonderful
vacation that could be yours with this limited time offer!
Blah...blah...blah."

I did, however, report the call to the police, hoping to save
another woman (who may or may not have been separated
from her husband) additional stress. I found the response
from the police somewhat shocking. They said that they
were pretty sure they knew who had made the call; he was
incarcerated but had phone privileges. Now, I have watched
a lot of movies. Usually, the alleged suspect gets one call and
calls his lawyer. (A call for pizza delivery or to connect with
an old girlfriend might be legal, but would be ill-advised.)
Allowing phone privileges in prison? Multiple, unsupervised
calls? Perhaps the local police force was focusing on larger
community crime issues.

What kind of inmate used his time to make sleazy phone
calls? I supposed that had he been a good decision-maker, he
might not be in prison. If he watched the same prison movies
I did, he would be spending his time doing in-place exercises
to build his body! He would be studying birds that landed
outside his cell window. He would be reading.

There was a time in my life when I thought that it would be
lovely to be in prison and have uninterrupted blocks of time
for myself. I was a single mother of a five-year-old. I was

teaching full time, going to graduate school at night, taking ballet classes (only because the night of my graduate classes, I had a babysitter), and spending what little time remained preparing for my teaching classes by reading young-adult fiction or the essays of the thirteen-year-olds in my charge.

Perhaps I loved being both a mother and a teacher. Perhaps I was too busy to think prison a realistic option. I hadn't ever taken the time to seriously consider what it would be like to use prison-issued shampoo (probably without conditioner) and interact in close quarters with individuals whose company I might not prefer. I'll never know because I never went to prison and my daughter grew up to be a competent, loving person.

Life has a way of working out. After teaching all those years, I am now retired and finally have some time for myself. I avoid in-place or any other kind of exercise. I take pleasure in watching birds gather in my backyard but hardly ever study them. I do read. I write. I play with the dogs. I spend my time – my own delicious time – exactly as I choose.

Winter Beach

Snow,
Whiter than bleached sand,
Drifts between straw sticks
And shiny stones.

A thousand faithful gulls
Shiver in February,
Held by mysterious tides and moon-secrets.

I will run crusty tracks across
Stilled surf,
Delight in the fresh wash of
Browns and grays,
And spend a child's hour in
A world of white light.

Skiing

"If I survive this," she thought, "I'm going to charge into that lodge and stand as close to the fire as I can without actually standing in it!" A gust of wind slapped her face, and she wondered why she was there. She had always hated the cold.

Two reassuring snaps of her bindings later, and she was hurrying to the chair. There was no line; the wind and biting cold would keep the meek huddled by the fire in the lodge today.

The edge of the seat slammed into the back of her knees, scooping her carelessly onto the icy surface. She and her partner-for-the-moment lowered the glazed safety bar. A few errant flakes chilled her nose, breath steaming up her goggles. Adjusting her scarf, she braced herself for the long ride up the mountain.

The chair swayed from occasional gusts, the frail ice-covered clamp clinging to the cable. She hoped it would hold. The ominous creaking of the chair as it passed each tower was the only sound.

The lone spacecraft floated onward in silence. A few minutes in, the daggers of frozen treetops almost reached to her seat. On the ground below, snow swirled across slabs of blue – wild ice rivers. New powder had blown into the woods. Her heart began to race. She decided not to look down.

The breath fogged her goggles, freezing almost instantly. She looked at her partner; motionless, he seemed frozen, too.

Suddenly, the chair jerked to a stop. After rocking slightly, all was still. Such a stop was annoying on a good day; today it might be dangerous.

They were far up the mountain; the terrain below was ragged. Would it even be possible for rescuers to position their equipment below and lower them down from the lifts?

The wind picked up. The chair swayed. She didn't think she could stand the cold another second.

Without warning, the chair jolted forward. No sooner had they started moving again when it was time to get off. Inching forward on the seat, they lifted ski tips, threw back the safety bar, and at the last possible moment, leaped onto the icy path, edges grabbing frozen ruts as they scrambled to balance.

The summit was deserted. The wind stung her face. Her breath, frozen in her scarf, chafed at her cheek. A boot needing adjustment would have to wait; the skiers moved quickly. Her thoughts turned to the lodge at the foot of the mountain and the race to warmth. She began to ski.

Further down, the wind abated. She had arrived to the quiet shelter of the glades. The splendor of this new world exploded before her. Each branch glittered with frost. A shower of white had fallen upon slopes, undisturbed but for the scattered tracks of a few other skiers.

As she carved arcs around buttery mounds and set soft rhythms in the stillness, she soon forgot the cruelty of the summit. Refreshing veils of snow tingled on her face. She danced in sunlight, and – quite suddenly – understood why she had come.

The Haircut

I was at the kitchen table, clipping coupons. We were on a budget and every little bit helped. My husband came in. He had just gotten a haircut. It was a terrible cut! The back, at the hairline, was cut straight across as if someone had used a bowl.

"Even I could do bett...." I started, but in the middle of my sentence, the skies opened and light poured down. Inspiration! If he would let me cut his hair, we would save at least $30 a pop. That's a lot of coupons! How hard could it be?

I already had the clippers. One of our dogs developed "hot spots" from scratching, and before each summer, I would always trim the hair around his neck. Come to think of it, these might even be clippers designed for human beings! Also, I had some experience cutting hair; I used to have a schnauzer. I was full of confidence, and my husband agreed that when he next needed a haircut, he would let me do it.

When the time arrived, I brought a chair into the bathroom. He sat down. I put a towel around his neck just like they do in salons. I cleared the area rug so that clean-up would be easier.

The clippers came in a special case with a little bottle of oil, a brush for maintenance, some scissors for fine trimming, and a series of guards for the blades. Each of the four guards determined how long the remaining hair would be: 1 inch, ½ inch, ¼ inch, and finally 1/8th of an inch. We chose the ¼-inch guard to start and I attached it to the blade.

I started from his neck and worked my way up, making sure to taper carefully so he wouldn't have that dreaded bowl look. I stopped every so often to brush the hair from his shoulders. He was losing a bit of hair right on top, and it was important that the transition from scalp to hair be gradual so he wouldn't look like Dilbert.

It was really going well. I had to remove the guard to cut the hair right above each ear, leaving a nice clean line. I took care of the stray hairs on his neck as well. I walked around to face him and admire my work. It was just about perfect...except for one little area to the left that was just a bit too long. I decided that with one more pass up that side, we would be done.

I began again. Oops! I had forgotten to put the guard back on the blade. You'd be amazed how quickly that thing cut without the guard on! Before I knew it, I had cut a hole about the size of a quarter, and it went right down to his scalp. This was a problem. He couldn't go to work like that; people might think he had ringworm. The only way to correct it was to shave off the rest of his hair, but he didn't want to do that. He wasn't angry; he just groaned a lot.

This may sound crazy, but I thought I might be able to cover the spot with just a bit of spray paint. Unfortunately, it was Sunday night and the stores were closed. It would have been hard to match the exact color anyway.

In those days, people dressed rather formally for work. It was long before "casual Friday." We determined that even if he did wear a hat to work, eventually he would have to take it off.

He could walk a bit sideways, always keeping the offending side of his head to the wall, but people might think him odd. Sticking an explanatory note on his collar was also out of the question.

We finally decided that he would just tell each person he encountered, "My wife gave me this haircut." He expected to have to repeat this many times. *My wife gave me this haircut. My wife gave me this haircut.*

It actually worked out far better than we thought. The moment someone new entered the room, others would say, "His wife gave him that haircut."

I have been cutting his hair for more than thirty years now. Shortly after the incident, he would always interrupt me to ask, "Are you sure the guard is on? *Are you sure?*" It was quite annoying.

Now he only asks once in a while.

Hungry House

The hungry house calls out for
Sandpaper, wallpaper, paint.
On bended knee
We labor.

We are called from our rest.
We are called from our plans.
We are called from our intent.

Into the night
Door frames rain dust,
Walls absorb paint,
Hammers pound.

Tribute is given:
Our backs,
Our knuckles,
Our nails.

We dream.
Photo-bright rooms
Fill our fantasies.

Someday
We will settle into thick chairs,
Read by the fire,
Sip tea from warm mugs.

Someday
When the work is done.

The Slip

It is uncharacteristic of me to express emotion in public. It doesn't mean that nothing is going on inside of me; it just means that the casual observer won't know what it is. A colleague on a principal-search committee once described me as having "ice water in my veins." When I won the first prize in a furniture store drawing, a luxurious theater weekend in NYC, those who called to tell me were disappointed that they didn't have the expected elation to record for their radio audience.

Being clinical served me well in teaching. If you respond emotionally to a thirteen-year-old's misbehavior, he gains control of the situation and wins. In parent conferences as well, it is important to appear calm. Many people are particularly sensitive about their children and sometimes interpret comments as criticism of their parenting skills.

In fact, when I left teaching and moved into real estate, a manager told me that nurses and teachers do well in real estate because among other things, they can appear calm. This is an asset since real estate clients can also be very stressed; in some cases, the sale or purchase of a home represents their major financial holding. Be they buyer or seller, each party can become very emotional.

One time, I received a phone call from an irate client. "I went to a party and another real estate agent said to me, 'You must be the client from Hell!' It must have come from you!" I was shocked. I made a point of never discussing clients with

50

other agents...and it just wasn't something I would say. (For a moment, though, I wondered if the client had read my mind.) She must not have really believed that I had said it because she re-signed with me shortly thereafter.

A good real estate agent will share the executive summary of complications with the client in order to spare him additional stress, then work "behind the scenes" to remove obstacles to the transaction. There are *always* obstacles: roof issues, electrical issues, plumbing issues, furnace issues, financial issues, and more. When a client wanted to buy a home owned by a church and we discovered that each person on the original church committee had died, I had to negotiate with the eleven people in the new committee since they each needed to agree to the sale. Another time, when a furnace failed two days before a closing, my client was ecstatic that I had negotiated a new furnace rather than a repair. In each case, calm demeanor had been necessary to accomplish the goal.

One day, as I rushed around in my car between appointments, I called a client to review some final details before an upcoming closing. It was a busy day for me, and I decided to do a personal errand on the way. When the business concluded, I turned my attention to pulling into the parking lot of Home Depot. As you may know, all lanes in the lot are for two-way traffic, except for the first to the immediate left. I noticed a parking spot two cars in from where I was. Though I knew it was a one-way lane, no cars were coming and I was in a hurry. I pulled in.

Another driver noticed what I had done and leaned out his truck window to shout, "Do you know what you're doing?" in a demeaning tone. Annoyed, I shouted back, "Fuck you! I know what I'm doing!" I don't know if he even heard me, but my client, who was still on the line since I hadn't disconnected properly – did.

I heard a sound, perhaps static – or, to my horror, someone clearing his throat – and then a long silence.

When I could manage to speak again, I said, "I'm so sorry! I'm pulling into a parking lot and someone just criticized my driving. I wasn't speaking to you." Another long silence. What could he be thinking? I had seen transactions fall apart for little things. Once I had a sale in jeopardy because the seller learned that the buyer intended to chop down her favorite tree!

Was the client now wondering if my professionalism had been a sham all along? Was his opinion of me shattered? Would he complain to my manager? Would I be reprimanded? Was my job in jeopardy?

Suddenly, I heard laughter. "Oh, Ann, I'm so relieved. I thought you were angry with *me*!"

Intention

Glancing up through brick-red
Tradition of a courtyard,
My eyes catch on one white speck as it
Dances.

Soft flakes drift,
Swirl in patterns,
Settle softly on my hair.

I strain to mark a pattern,
Some order in the fall,
A suggestion of His hand,
Evidence of intention.

Thoughts stray to the sea shell,
The spider web,
Other things perhaps planned.

The moment breathes softly
Without testament.
Nothing more is required.

Perception

Young.
Railing against
Injustice,
Cruelty,
Suffering.

Later.
Speaking about
Motives,
Behaviors,
Consequences.

Gaining
Experience.

Developing
Philosophy,
Faith,
Wisdom.

Changing.
Learning to accept,
Without understanding,
A world so flawed.

Modern Poetry

Her first love,
The patterns and music,
The language of verse,

The poetry of rhyme
Passing into shadow with
Melodies of Gershwin and Porter.
Her words speak her own time.

Each generation
Reflects times less forgiving,
Steps beyond gentle.

New poets slam,
Scream in discord.
Music cuts sharp,
No longer familiar.

Her audience now,
Those who love her,
Who smile and nod,
Even when they never spoke
The language.

To Remember

I watch leaves edged in gold
Fall,
Float,
Slip into the stream,
Drifting beyond my reach.

I strain to capture
Crisp images in memory
So that
When the last of the leaves
Has disappeared from sight,
I will remember you.

Bury Her

Bury her with sharpened pencils.
Don't forget the stake through her heart.
She will want to get some rest.

ANN ROUSSEAU received her undergraduate and graduate degrees from the University of Connecticut and Fairfield University, respectively. She taught English in exemplary middle schools in New Canaan and Darien, Connecticut, for thirty-three years. During her tenure in Darien, she served as Curriculum Monitor for English at Middlesex Middle School. She was a Fellow of the Connecticut Writing Project in 1986 and studied briefly with Irish Poet Laureate Paula Meehan as part of the Paris Writers Workshop in 2002. Her first book, *Barefoot: A Collection of Poems*, is available on Amazon.com. She lives in Connecticut with her husband and two golden retrievers, and enjoys spending time with her two granddaughters.

www.ingramcontent.com/pod-product-compliance
Lightning Source LLC
Chambersburg PA
CBHW060135260626
47160CB00005B/2115